Preparing Morning and Evening Prayer

James Richards

NOVALIS
THE LITURGICAL PRESS

Design: Eye-to-Eye Design, Toronto

Layout: Suzanne Latourelle

Illustrations: Eugene Kral

Series Editor: Bernadette Gasslein

© 1997, Novalis, Saint Paul University, Ottawa, Ontario, Canada

Business Office: Novalis, 49 Front Street East, 2nd floor, Toronto, Ontario M5E 1B3

Published in the United States of America by The Liturgical Press, Box 7500, Collegeville, MN 56321-7500

Novalis: ISBN 289088 802 9

The Liturgical Press: ISBN 0-8146-2516-9
A Liturgical Press Book
Library of Congress data available on request

Printed in Canada.

Richards, James, 1945

Preparing morning and evening prayer

(Preparing for liturgy)
Includes bibliographical references.
ISBN 2-89088-802-9

1. Public worship–Catholic Church. 2. Catholic Church–Liturgy. I. Title. II. Series

BX2000.R53 1997   264L0207   C97-900973-1

Contents

Introduction

In the early 1950s, I lived with my parents and other family members in a small fishing village where our lives centred around the parish church and local school. Besides Sunday mass and other weekday morning celebrations, we often returned to the church later on Sundays for the recitation of the rosary and benediction of the blessed sacrament. As an altar server—whether thurifer, candle bearer or master of ceremonies, I knew my duties very well. I knew the familiar hymns, "O Salutaris Hostia" and "Tantum Ergo" just as well. I was also most tempted to join the choir as we concluded with "Holy God, We Praise Thy Name." But singing was the choir's task, not mine. The ritual was quite simple: a combination of words, gestures and symbols whose format was almost always the same. The regular participants were very much at home with this half-hour of prayer and eucharistic devotion. We knew what would happen and what our participation was to be. Also, we knew it was a moment of encounter with God and that the presence of the Divine was especially experienced and celebrated there.

I also remember walking by the rectory and seeing our parish priest pacing back and forth along the veranda or the pathway to the church, black book in hand, silently reading or praying. He did it regularly, and the book was always close by. Well-worn, it was obviously very important to our pastor, but apparently only for him. He never read to us from the book or referred to it at any of the times of prayer in the church. Yes, he was reading the breviary, praying the divine office and therefore performing a "priestly duty" with great commitment and regularity.

Almost a half century later, much has happened in the liturgical tradition of many Christian communities, and the Roman Catholic Church in particular. In many cases, benediction of the blessed sacrament has been replaced by evening masses. The rosary, though still a popular devotion, does not occupy the dominant place it did some years ago. Prayer groups have become a source of spiritual growth for many people, whether they have sprung from movements in the church such as cursillo or the charismatic renewal. Following Vatican II, the book of the divine office was revised, translated and made into a contemporary prayer book for priests, deacons and a small number of other people who use it regularly.

One of Our Best Kept Secrets

We could stop there and leave the impression that this is all that has happened to the public prayer of the church since the Second Vatican Council.

If we do so, we would miss a very important part of liturgical renewal because one of the best kept secrets of the reform of the liturgy is the *General Instruction on the Liturgy of the Hours (GILH)*. This document, promulgated by the Sacred Congregation For Divine Worship in 1971, has called us as church to be a people of prayer, to recognize that, through baptism, we have a serious responsibility to pray the prayer of the church, to intercede for the world, to offer praise to our God and to grow in holiness as God's people.

So far, we have failed to take up the challenge, and the liturgy of the hours has remained the prayer form of a very small minority of Catholics. The purpose of this book is to take the *General Instruction on the Liturgy of the Hours*, along with the history of prayer of the church, and place before you practical ways to implement this form of liturgical prayer in the life of your community.

Let us look at the opening lines of the *GILH*: "The public and communal prayer of the people of God is rightly considered among the first duties of the Church. From the very beginning the baptised 'remain faithful to the teaching of the apostles, to the brotherhood, to the breaking of bread and to the prayers' (Acts 2:42)" [1]. "These prayers in common gradually took on a more definite shape, which today we describe as 'the course of the Hours.' This Liturgy of the Hours, or Divine Office, further enriched with readings, is principally a prayer of praise and supplication, indeed it is the prayer of the Church with Christ and to Christ" [2].

The Nature of This Prayer

That the prayer of the church described in the document is both public and communal, that it belongs to all members of the faithful, cannot be overstated. Every member of the church has a serious responsibility to pray the prayer of the church. The Jewish and Christian scriptures form the basis of our tradition of prayer. The book of psalms, among other Old Testament writings, clearly indicates that our tradition of regular prayer times predates Christianity. But in the Christian context, our prayer takes place in and through Christ. Jesus Christ intercedes before the Father, as the one and eternal priest for all humanity. Our prayer is always through Christ as he is our access to the one eternal God. For Christians, the source of such prayer is the action of the Holy Spirit who unites God's people, the church, and leads us through Christ to the Father. So, like all Christian prayer, the liturgy of the hours is trinitarian.

As in the celebration of the eucharist and other sacraments, we celebrate who we are as Christians, a people immersed into the paschal mystery. In the liturgy of the hours, we celebrate that we are raised up to new life through the passion, death and resurrection of Jesus Christ. Since Vatican II, we have become more aware that every sacramental celebration immerses us in the paschal mystery. It is important for us to see how this same paschal faith is celebrated in these other times of public liturgical prayer. Hopefully this will become even more obvious through the use of this book.

Morning and Evening Prayer

The two most common times of prayer for Christians are morning and evening. Traditionally they were called Lauds and Vespers, but names are not the most important issue. The vocation to be a people of prayer, "to pray constantly," invites us to use these two specific times as the hinges of the day. The beginning of the day is a call to praise, to bless our God for the new day set before us. It is a time to be renewed as God's people, to recognize that we belong to the risen Christ. The psalmody of the day often reflects this.

Evening prayer changes emphasis slightly: it is a time of thanksgiving, a moment to review the day and ask forgiveness for the ways we may have failed to practise the teaching of Jesus during the past twenty-four hours. As the day draws to a close, we ask our God for a peaceful sleep and a restful night.

In Summary

1. From our Jewish ancestry, Christians have inherited a tradition of public liturgical prayer. Though language and cultural adaptations have changed it over time, its consistent basis is prayer offered to our God through Christ, the one priest. It is the celebration of our immersion into the death and resurrection of Jesus Christ, the paschal mystery.

2. Christians are urged to pray constantly, but the two traditional prayer times are morning, a time of praise, and evening, a time of thanksgiving and asking for forgiveness. They are sometimes called "the hinges of the day."

Discussion Questions

1. Describe your experience of public communal prayer thus far.

2. Is the statement from the *GILH* on page 6 regarding prayer a realistic goal for the church in the twenty-first century? Why or why not?

3. Discuss prayer outside the eucharist as an immersion into the paschal mystery.

CHAPTER 1

A Short History

The Jewish synagogue at the time of Jesus was the place where the community gathered for prayer and reflection on the word of God. The psalms were an integral part of the prayer of the Hebrew people, as they are still.

Jesus taught the disciples to pray both by word and example. The gospels speak of Jesus praying the psalms with the disciples at the last supper (Mark 14:26), and even in the last moments on the cross, they form his prayer of abandonment: "My God, my God, why have you forsaken me?" (Mark 15:34); "Father, into your hands, I commend my Spirit" (Luke 23:46). The Acts of the Apostles speak of the members of the Christian community as those who "remained faithful to the teaching of the apostles, to the brotherhood, to the breaking of bread and to the prayers"(2:42). In his letters Saint Paul tells his readers to pray always (Ephesians 5:18). Other New Testament writings also indicate that the psalms were considered central to the prayer life of the community (e.g. Col 3:16). In the first decades of the church, Christians prayed in the synagogues with other members of the Jewish community. By the turn of the first century, however, they had left that community, either by force or choice, and were on their own.

There was no one style of prayer in the church of the first centuries after Christ. People prayed publicly and privately, in small groups and as families. One characteristic, however, marked the theology of prayer. A person prayed as a member of the church, as part of the body of Christ. The concept of "me and my God" was foreign to the early Christians. Prayer, even in its most private and personal expressions, was always an experience of praying with and for others.

East and West

In different areas of the east and west, various styles of prayer were beginning to develop. For instance, in the east, the desert monks of upper and lower Egypt used the psalms as their normal prayer and some had developed a style of praying the whole psalter, the 150 psalms, every day. We can only wonder if this was one more example of "more being better," a trap into which people can fall in our time as well. Other groups prayed the psalter over the course of a week. In monasteries, both in the east (Asia Minor and North Africa) and west (Rome, France and Spain), other forms of psalm-based prayer rituals were developing.

But not all of this was happening in monasteries. A form of regular prayer was also taking place in the main church of the area. This so-called "cathedral office" was different from the monastic model. Here, the bishop usually presided, and parishioners saw this as a regular part of their faith life. Instead of trying to pray many psalms and changing them continually, this form was based on a style of repetition; people took part whether or not they could read. Cantors would lead the people in singing, and the use of light and incense were part of the prayer.

William Storey, in an article entitled "Liturgy of the Hours: Cathedral versus Monastery"(*Christians at Prayer*, John Gallen, S.J., editor [University of Notre Dame Press: 1977], 61-82), describes six characteristics of this formal liturgical prayer:

- They were, as obligatory prayers, an affair for the whole local church, with the participation of lay and ordained, and a commonplace part of the religious observance of daily life.
- They were christological in intent and content. Morning prayer celebrated the resurrection of Jesus and evening prayer centred on his burial and descent among the dead. The author refers to an early Christian writer, Hippolytus, who made connections between the events of the passion of Jesus and times of prayer throughout the day.
- The hours were composed of christological psalms and hymns with some Old Testament psalms and extended intercessory prayer.

- Daily services were highly structured and almost totally invariable. This was not the place for either spontaneous or loosely structured prayer, which was not the custom of the time.
- The prayer was seen, not as instructive or edifying, but as a time of praise, thanksgiving, adoration and worship. Seldom is scripture reading or preaching a part of the format.
- It was episcopal and popular. Although it was highly clerical, as the bishop normally presided and a number of priests and deacons were present, it was also popular, as many people participated in it. The simplicity and unchanging structure allowed them to feel included in the ritual. The responsorial style of praying the psalmody was an important part of this. The cantor intoned the antiphon, the people joined in and the cantor sang the verses of the psalm. There was no need for books or papers simply because these were a rare commodity and many of the participants could not read.

Fulfilling the Role of Being Church

The motives for such prayer were also to fulfill the role of being church: to praise God and intercede for the world. This contrasts to the monastic style, which was much more centred on spiritual formation, to make one more holy. In the cathedral (or pastoral) office the use of rituals such as processions and bowing, and of symbols such as candle and incense indicates that this liturgy is composed of more than words.

While people were encouraged to pray always, morning and evening became the normal prayer times for the cathedral office. There was also a resurrection vigil on Sunday mornings which, over the centuries, dropped out of regular use. Later, only at times of special vigils such as Easter were more extensive prayer offices celebrated.

Clericalization of the Prayer of the Church

Another change was taking place in the prayer of the church. As the church moved into the Middle Ages (the sixth century and following), the liturgy in general, which included the divine office, became the domain of clerics and was not seen as something in which the faithful needed to actively partake. The result was that clerics (bishops, priests and deacons) were obligated to pray the office in the name of the church. Because many of these did not live in community, they received permission to pray the office alone. Monks and nuns in monasteries prayed in common but used a different format from that of the cathedral church.

In the process, the cathedral office almost disappeared. Whenever there were attempts to revive this prayer form, the monastic style was always used as the model. So secular priests and everyone else used some form of prayer based on the monastic office. This included many psalms and readings, but few intercessory prayers. Even in cathedrals where there was a tradition of praying the office, the task was performed by a group of clerics commissioned for it. While the faithful might attend, they were unable to participate because the prayer was said or sung in Latin. Yet we can be sure that there was a deep yearning on the part of the laity to come in touch with their Lord through an experience of communal prayer, for prayer, as a corporate experience, is deeply rooted in the Judeo-Christian faith tradition.

Now, with this brief background, let us look in a little more detail at the Vatican II teaching on the subject and what we are called to do to bring this form of public liturgical prayer into the mainstream of church life.

In Summary

1. The psalms and canticles of the Jewish scriptures were a normal part of the prayer of Jesus, his disciples and the members of the church in the first centuries.

2. In the monasteries of both East and West, as well as the cathedral churches, there developed a variety of formats for public liturgical prayer. All members of the faithful regularly participated in these times of prayer, especially in the cathedral or pastoral setting.

3. During the Middle Ages, the public office became a clerical obligation and the lay faithful participated more by their presence than by their active involvement. This was also a time when many other devotional practices began to spring up as these faithful hungered for opportunities to pray together.

Discussion Questions

1. What is your most treasured style of prayer? Does it take place with other people or by yourself?

2. Four types of prayer are prayer of praise, petition and thanksgiving and prayer for mercy. Do all of these form a rhythm in your prayer? Reflect and discuss.

3. Discuss together the importance of praying (interceding) for the needs of the world. Do you perceive this as part of our Christian vocation?

CHAPTER 2

Renewing the Pastoral Office: *The General Instruction*

Let us now look at some of the content of the *General Instruction on the Liturgy of the Hours*, promulgated by the Sacred Congregation for Divine Worship on February 2, 1971. It forms the basis of the renewal of public liturgical prayer apart from the celebration of the sacraments. The document stresses that this prayer of the church does not belong exclusively to clerics or monastics, but is the prayer of all the faithful, the public prayer of the church. While there may have been attempts, such as Sunday vespers in the parish, to celebrate some parts of this prayer for larger groups, people never saw it as having anything to do with them. With the advent of evening masses, this too was left aside.

Many Catholics may remember seeing priests reading from their breviary whenever they had an idle moment; the book was a constant companion. Perhaps we saw it as admirable but we knew that it had nothing to do with us; it was the priest's role to pray for the rest of us or, perhaps even more, for his personal sanctification. While the document stresses the responsibility of ordained ministers and monastics to pray the liturgy of the hours, the mandate is much wider:

> The church, united with Christ, the mediator, intercedes for the world, prays for the needs of all, offers worship to the loving creator... Our Lord Jesus Christ prays for us, prays in us, and is prayed to by us. ... The whole body of the Church shares in the priesthood of Christ. The baptised, by regeneration and the anointing of the Holy Spirit, are consecrated into a spiritual house and a holy priesthood (7).

The Liturgy of the Hours, like all other liturgical services, is not a private function, but pertains to the whole body of the church. It manifests the church and has an effect on it. Its ecclesial celebration is best seen and especially recommended when it is performed—with the bishop surrounded by his priests and ministers—by the local church, 'in which the one true, catholic and apostolic church of Christ is truly present and operative' (20).

Whenever possible, the more important hours could be celebrated in common at the church (21).

It is most fitting that permanent deacons should recite some part of the Liturgy of the Hours each day as determined by the episcopal conference (30).

The first chapter of the five in the document gives the background and theology of the liturgy of the hours. The following chapters speak about the structure and parts of the prayer. Chapter five speaks of the different ministers involved in this "public and communal prayer" of the church, as well as of singing the office.

Sometimes it seems that a number of people with different ideas put this document together. The actual book, the four-volume *The Liturgy of the Hours* or the one-volume *Christian Prayer*, is rather cumbersome and appears to be designed for individual reading or monastic use. While the document clearly encourages all the faithful to pray the liturgy of the hours, the resulting structure makes this difficult. It is not easily adapted for use in the parish.

There have been some very good attempts to bridge this gap. Hymn books such as *Gather* and *Praise God in Song* offer a variety of formats for praying this public prayer of the church. In Canada we have one of the most up-to-date resources for this prayer as presented in *Catholic Book of Worship III*. It provides detailed formats for morning prayer (13A-I) and evening prayer (14A-M). Additional hymns and psalms that are directly related to these prayer times are found in numbers 649 to 687. But that is just a beginning because *Catholic Book of Worship III* is more than an ordinary hymn book: it is a resource for the whole liturgical activity of the parish. Besides the responsorial psalms, which are easily adapted for the liturgy of the hours, it includes a variety of settings for psalms and canticles. As we become more accustomed to this valuable resource, hopefully we will experience the liturgy of the hours as a regular part of the public prayer of the church. Perhaps the day will come when every parish will offer opportunities for morning and evening prayer at least once a week, and others may celebrate it every day. On weekdays when there is no mass, morning or evening prayer is a much better choice for the people who wish to gather. This requires some planning and even a change of mentality. Yet if we don't start, it will never happen. The celebration of the word and distribution of communion is properly a service for Sundays when it is not possible to celebrate mass.

To Gather the People

We have discussed that gathering for morning and evening prayer is not just an option for parish prayer, but a responsibility of the community. But it isn't what we are accustomed to. We do not come together on a regular basis for prayer unless it is for eucharist. If Marian devotions, the recitation of the rosary and benediction of the blessed sacrament were popular forms of prayer and devotion prior to the Vatican II, very little has replaced them.

We tend to use the mass as the one form of prayer for all occasions because it is possible to celebrate eucharist at any time of day. The recent custom of celebrating eucharist much more often and on many different occasions has been a blessing in some ways, but is problematic in others. While the liturgical reforms of the mass may have de-mystified certain aspects of the celebration, they have also allowed people to buy into a consumer mentality. Unless they receive something, in this case, holy communion, they may feel that they didn't get anything out of it. We need to study this phenomenon, but, for now, suffice it to say that, for many Catholic Christians, gathering simply to praise and thank God and pray for the world's needs does not seem to be enough. Perhaps the great exception to this is charismatic prayer groups which do attract many people to prayer in a variety of forms. Yet we also know that this particular style of prayer is not necessarily for everyone. Nor is it liturgical prayer in a formal sense, precisely because it lacks its structure and style. The two forms are not incompatible, but are rather quite different expressions of the same call to offer praise to God and intercede on behalf of the world.

What can we do as parish liturgical teams and committees to gather people for morning and evening prayer? What will convince parishioners that morning praise or evening psalmody are good ways to enter more deeply into the paschal mystery? Some background work needs to be done.

First, pastoral teams need to be convinced that it is a worthwhile endeavour. They will need to look at the different ministries involved and choose people who have both the gifts and skills to best serve the community. This will be discussed in detail later.

Consider the current mass schedule in the parish. Is there a celebration of mass every day, twice a day, or on Sunday evening? In many Catholic dioceses, there are fewer priests in parishes. This may mean, among other things, a need to reduce the number of weekday masses and change the schedule. How do we see this? Is it a negative tendency in the worship life of our parishes or an opportunity to call the faithful to a different way of praying that is also an authentic part of our faith tradition? In communities accustomed to a regular schedule of weekday masses, a reduction in the number of masses is indeed an adjustment. Any regular liturgical celebration or other devotional practice that has "always been there"—and now it is not—means that the faithful of that community will suffer some pain in adapting to a different schedule. These anchors of prayer and personal reflection give people something to hold on to when many other things in their lives are in a state of flux. Yet, to be able to come together for a time of prayer, to reflect on the word of God, to experience the presence of the Lord in different ways can truly be a source of strength and encouragement to many members of the church.

The important question for Catholics may be: "Is the mass the only beneficial way to gather in church for prayer?" Is it necessary to receive the eucharist each time we are called to celebrate, both personally and communally, the presence of the

Lord in our lives? One of the great insights of the *Constitution on the Sacred Liturgy* is that there are four modes of the presence of Christ in the liturgy: in the gathering of the faithful, that is, the assembly; in the presider; in the proclamation of the word of God and in the eucharist. How important that we grow in our knowledge and appreciation of these various aspects of Christ's presence among us! When people gather to pray morning and evening prayer in the parish church as a public act of worship, Christ's presence is just as real as in the eucharistic assembly. Those present are gathered in Christ's name; therefore he is present among them. The presider, ordained or lay, has the ministry of welcoming all in the name of Christ. In the word of God proclaimed in the assembly, Christ is speaking to his people in that time and place. This is no casual gathering, but a true act of worship that celebrates Christ the Lord, present among us. It is our proclamation of the paschal mystery.

When to Introduce This Prayer

When is a good time to introduce this prayer to the parish? A number of communities find that one of the two preparation seasons, Advent or Lent, can be a time of heightened awareness of our need to reconnect with a more consistent life of prayer.

The season of Advent has a spirit of beginning anew and preparing for both the Lord's return at the end time and the feast of Christmas. Even though our society has made Advent a time of celebration of the feast we are anticipating, we can still be somewhat counter-cultural by offering people a regular time of prayer.

The season of Lent calls us to a spirit of repentance and conversion. To offer a time of morning and evening prayer at the most convenient hour for the parish could make the difference that moves the people of your community beyond an individual experience of repentance to a communal recognition of the Lord's healing love. Again, when the community does not celebrate mass on Sunday night, this is an ideal time to invite the community to gather to prayerfully conclude the Lord's Day with evening prayer.

With the *GILH*, the church calls us to make this prayer again the normal form of communal public prayer in mornings and evenings, during the week and on Sunday evenings.

Characteristics of Liturgical Prayer

It is ecclesial, communal, structured and has an objective character (it is theocentric and done for a specific reason). The church prays because Christ prays. We continue the mission and ministry of Christ in our prayer. We do so, not out of obligation, but because we recognize who we are, the body of Christ. It is our nature to be people of prayer. Prayer best expresses the very essence of the church as community. It is a real union effected by the Holy Spirit, for there can be no community prayer without the Spirit's action. It is a real act of worship. Christ is present among us when we pray as Church: "Where two or three are gathered ...".

A Basic Format

Let us take a quick glance at the basic format of communal prayer as it normally happens in parishes and other communities today. This format, with nine possible elements, makes up morning and evening prayer.

1. Gathering: At the parish church or smaller chapel depending on the size of the assembly. A room with flexible seating can sometimes be helpful.

2. Greeting: The presider begins with the formal liturgical greeting. As always, this is not a time for casual or informal talk. The presider, by baptism, represents Christ who calls us to prayer as members of his body.

3. Thanksgiving for Light (evening): More effective if everyone lights a taper from the evening candle.

4. Hymn: The common morning and evening hymns except for feasts or strong seasons (Advent/Christmas and Lent/Easter) are always the best choice.

5. Psalmody: The number varies from the one to three, including the standard psalm (morning, psalm 63 or evening, psalm 141), a second psalm (may be a seasonal psalm) and/or a canticle.

6. Reading: A non-gospel text from the Jewish or Christian scriptures.

7. Gospel canticle: Zechariah: Luke 1:68-79 (morning) and Mary: Luke 1:46-55 (evening).

8. Intercessions: Normally sung by the assistant or cantor.

9. Our Father: May be sung or recited with the concluding doxology.

10. Blessing and sign of peace: The conclusion of the prayer. There is no formal recessional.

Four or five ministries—presider, assistant, cantor, reader, thurifer—are possible for communal prayer or pastoral office. We will return to a fuller discussion of these components and ministries further on in this book. Now let us look at the psalms which are the core content of morning and evening prayer.

In Summary

1. The *General Instruction on the Liturgy of the Hours* is both a call to renewal of liturgical prayer and an outline about how we may bring the practice of this prayer to all the faithful.

2. Among the various formats available for the sung pastoral office, *Catholic Book of Worship III* presents one of the most up-to-date versions available; its psalmody, canticles and other hymns offer a great variety of possibilities.

3. The implementation of morning and evening prayer in the parish setting requires a strong commitment by the pastoral leaders and the liturgical committee. Strong liturgical seasons such as Advent and Lent may be ideal times to introduce this prayer to the community. Like all liturgy, this prayer continues the ministry of Christ in our time.

Discussion Questions

1. Besides the celebration of eucharist, is your parish community ready to pray publicly on a regular basis? What needs to be done for them to realize their priestly vocation of prayer?

2. Do the members of your parish recognize that Christ is present by their very gathering? In the presider? in the word proclaimed? Is there need for ongoing formation/education in this area? Whose work is this?

CHAPTER 3

The Psalmody

What are these prayers, the psalms? The one hundred and fifty psalms that comprise their own book in the Jewish scriptures are a most interesting series of prayers that are, at the same time, poems and songs. Sometimes considered creations of King David, they run the gamut of emotion and expression of prayer in the Jewish faith tradition. In some of the psalms we hear the voice of a single person and, at other times, they voice the corporate prayer of a whole community or nation. Sometimes they offer praise to God just to put things in perspective: God is God and we are not. They help the community acknowledge what that right relationship needs to be: creatures exalting the Creator with every ounce of their energy and with the best words they can find to express it.

In general we can categorize the psalms into three main groups: hymns of praise, lament (both individual and communal) and instruction. In these prayers we encounter acclamations of praise when the psalmist recognizes that ultimately everything comes from the kindness and mercy of God.

Sometimes the psalms of lament carry us to the depths of despair and invite us to identify with the one who feels abandoned and rejected by everyone, including God. But such prayers normally conclude with the psalmist calling out to God, acknowledging that, when no one else is there, the Lord's presence and love alone sustain the one who experiences desolation and fear. Psalm 130 is a good example of such a prayer. The psalmist begins with a plea to God for help, "Out of the depths I cry to you, O Lord." In verse seven we hear the confident declaration that indeed God will show forgiveness and grant redemption to the whole nation: "O Israel, hope in the Lord! For with the Lord there is steadfast love, and with him is the great power to redeem ..." (NRSV).

In his book, Two Ways of Praying (Nashville: Abingdon Press, 1995), Paul Bradshaw states that the church in the first centuries considered the psalms to be a very important and loved part of the scriptures. They had four principal beliefs about the focus of these prayers:

- they were written by King David;
- he was especially inspired by the Holy Spirit in this special work;
- the psalms were prophetic in the same way as the writing of the great prophets;
- they were messianic and christological.

As Bradshaw notes, "the verses of the psalms spoke about the Messiah, or were addressed to the Messiah or were words of the Messiah" (74). This is true in many of the books of the New Testament, especially the gospels and Acts of the Apostles. Perhaps the most dramatic examples are offered by the words of Jesus from the cross: "My God, my God, why have you forsaken me" (Mark 15:34), or "Father, into your hands I commend my spirit" (Luke 23:46). If we were to quickly peruse the gospels, we would see that there are numerous examples when verses of the psalms refer to Jesus as Messiah, helping the reader to understand how the evangelist recognized Jesus as the Christ and the fulfillment of the messianic hopes of the people.

Varied Geographies, Different Uses of Psalms

In different geographical areas, as the church's style of prayer continued to develop in the first centuries, variations on the use of psalms and non-biblical prayers and songs emerged. There were movements away from formal psalmody in communal prayer, and then a strong inclination to use only the one hundred and fifty canonical psalms as part of communal prayer in both the monastic and cathedral settings. If we can learn one thing from this, it is that either extreme is unnecessary.

Nourished by the Psalms

The psalms are integral to the Judeo-Christian heritage, and our lives are nourished as we use these inspired prayers. Their depth of poetic expression can carry us to the heights of praise and allow us to enter into a deeper realization of the mystery of the presence of God. To appreciate the poetry in English translation, I recommend a copy of the *Psalms for Morning and Evening Prayer* (Chicago: Liturgy Training Publications, 1996). This new translation from the International Commission on English in the Liturgy has done good work in bringing the richness of the psalmody into the language of our day; it will be of great benefit to English-speaking Christians.

Yes, there are one hundred and fifty psalms; to keep a good balance, however, we need not use all of them. Some do not easily adapt to morning and evening prayer, even if they may be helpful in personal reflection. Liturgical planners will need to have a certain flexibility in the choice of psalmody so that they best serve the community as it gathers to praise God.

Canticles

Besides the psalms, other prayers found throughout the Jewish and Christian scriptures have been part of morning and evening prayer. These canticles, including those of Zechariah and Mary in Luke 1, are in the form of praise and thanksgiving and joyfully acknowledge God's presence. George Guiver indicates some of the scripture references of these canticles in *Company of Voices* (New York: Pueblo, 1988). This partial list may help in planning for prayer:

Daniel 3:57-88 (Benedicite)
Isaiah 12:1-6
Isaiah 38:10-20
1 Samuel 2:1-10
Exodus 15:1-19
Habakkuk 3:2-19
Deuteronomy 32:1-43.

In its index *Catholic Book of Worship III* lists nine canticles with a variety of musical settings. Including a canticle or a psalm such as 117 after the other two psalms rounds out the prayer and brings that section before the reading to a more joyful conclusion. With good planning and practice, the musical settings to these canticles will definitely enhance the experience of prayer for the whole assembly.

In the history of liturgical prayer, one great hymn, the *Te Deum*, stands out as a classic canticle that offers praise to our God. It is recommended for use on Sundays and Feast Days. Trinitarian in focus, it speaks especially of the persons of the Father and Jesus, the Son. Bishop Raymond Lahey's new metrical translation of this ancient text, set to the well-known Welsh hymn tune, CWM RHONDDA, is found in the *Living With Christ Sunday Missal* (Ottawa: Novalis) and is included on page 43 of this book. Using this canticle certainly adds a special note of praise to our prayer.

In Summary

1. The 150 psalms offer a great variety of prayerful expression. They may be categorized into three main types, praise, lament and instruction. The early church considered the psalms to be about Christ, the Messiah. Choosing appropriate psalms for public prayer is a special work of planning groups.

2. Besides the psalms, the canticles constitute another group of prayers, some from scripture and others from tradition. These songs/poems add a special note of praise.

Discussion Questions

1. Prayerfully read aloud psalm 63 or psalm 141. After a time of silence, invite each participant to share a brief reflection on this psalm.

2. Use this same process to reflect on the Canticles of Zechariah (Benedictus) and Mary (Magnificat) as well as the *Te Deum*, "Praise Is Yours, O God, Forever."

CHAPTER 4

The Essentials of the Pastoral Office

"Where two or three are gathered in my name, I am there among them." The most important focus in praying the liturgy of the hours is that we come together. If the first manifestation of Christ's presence in the celebration of the eucharist is the assembly, this is true in all liturgical gatherings. When members of the Christian community assemble to pray, Christ is present because we gather in his name. If the only thing we are able to do as a community is simply pray a psalm, listen to the word of God and pray for the world, we have done what we are called to do and have exercised our vocation as a priestly people. Perhaps such a simple time of prayer may have lifted our spirits, brought us consolation, or helped us discern more clearly where the Lord is calling us as disciples. But that is not the reason for the gathering. No! It is to give praise to God and to intercede for the world. It is based firmly on the belief that prayer has power and that there is a greater power in prayer when we do it together. Such simple prayer also acknowledges that God is the creator of all and helps us to deepen our faith in God's steadfast love for all people. So, first, we need to come together for we need each other to be a community of faith in the risen Lord.

Another essential element of the pastoral office is ministry. We gather as people blessed with different gifts, including those needed to pray as community. Every ministry is important in the liturgical assembly, whether it be presider, assistant, cantor, lector or thurifer. (There is a discussion in some circles concerning the use of the terms "presider" or "leader" in liturgical prayer. Does the term "presider" refer only to a person who is ordained: bishop, priest or deacon? Does the term refer to any person who oversees any public gathering? The question will not be resolved here. I will use the term "presider" for that person who takes on the role of overall leadership of morning or evening prayer. During the prayer, a number of people exercise leadership at different times. The presider is one of them.)

Let us look at these ministries individually.

Presider

Who is called to lead prayer within the parish or other Christian community? The first standard is that this person should be a leader of the community. This means that the person is recognized as one who is intimately bound to the life of the community, and has earned the respect of the other members. While this person may be the ordained minister of the community, the presider at prayer does not require holy orders to exercise this ministry. Other pastoral leaders, by their presence in the community and their vocation of service to the faithful, may take on this ministerial role. Candidates for this liturgical ministry could include the chair of the parish pastoral council, the leader of the liturgical committee, or other natural leaders whom the parish recognizes as persons of deep faith and prayer. Such prayer leadership needs to be discerned by members of the pastoral team and/or liturgical committee.

What other qualities are needed? The presider is one who can comfortably stand before the community and, with confident gesture and voice, pray in the name of all those assembled. It is someone who feels comfortable robed in a simple baptismal alb, the vesture that belongs to all of us. It is a person who, by personal prayer and practice, becomes accustomed to the flow of the pastoral office and understands the different aspects of the prayer form. Finally, the presider is someone who does not bring a personal agenda to this ministry but is ready to listen to those responsible for its coordination. This prayer, like all liturgical prayer, belongs to the whole community, not just to those in leadership. It requires an openness to understand and be formed by the Holy Spirit working through this faith community.

The Assistant

In a way, every liturgical minister in the pastoral office is an assistant to the first minister, the assembly. This specific ministry may perform different tasks, depending on the structure of the prayer. For the smooth flow of the prayer, the presider prays the psalm prayers and concluding prayer with arms outstretched (called the *orans* posture). The assistant, without blocking the view of the assembly, stands to the right of the presider, and holds the book so that the presider can easily read it. The assistant's ministry is essential so that the presider's book is open at the right place and time. At evening prayer, the assistant may carry the candle into the assembly and sing the evening thanksgiving after the presider proclaims the opening words. As well, this person may also lead the people in the intercessions of both morning and evening prayer. The assistant's ministry may not require singing, but should allow the presider to lead well. But it may also call for the talent to sing some parts of the liturgy. Like the presider, the assistant needs to be able to follow the direction of those responsible for the prayer and have a good understanding of the format.

The Cantor

This ministry, lost to the life of the assembly for centuries, has an essential role today. The task of this ministry is to proclaim the responsorial psalm in any liturgy of the word, including eucharist. Psalms are made for singing, whether in the original Hebrew or in their modern translations. As well, the canticles from both the Jewish and Christian scriptures are much more clearly expressed as prayer when they have a musical setting. Singing the responsorial psalm takes priority over gathering and closing hymns at eucharist. (The entrance and communion antiphons that are part of the proper prayers at mass, while not used much in the liturgy today, indicate that a cantor would lead the assembly in an appropriate psalm at those times as well. Simply reciting them at the beginning of mass or during the communion rite does not indicate their true meaning.) The cantor thus serves a kind of dual role: as a minister of music and of the word, blending them together in proclamation and prayer so that the whole assembly is raised up in spirit to praise God.

Therefore, the cantor needs to develop gifts and skills in two areas. Some knowledge of and ability to read music is a benefit. While this is helpful, it is not essential. Practising with the parish music director or other pastoral musicians in learning psalm tones and musical settings can bring forth many talented parishioners who do not read music. Many musical settings of psalmody for use in parishes are recorded on cassette tapes. The National Liturgical Office of the Canadian Catholic Conference of Bishops has published a series of these cassettes through its Publications Service. These good quality cassettes cover much of the newer music in *Catholic Book of Worship III*. Having a sensitivity to or an ear for music and the desire to further their skills will help people develop this ministry.

Much of the cantor's role is to sing the verses of the psalms so that the assembly can make these words their own in prayer. The better this is done, the more prayerful is the gathering. This does not mean that the cantor need be a professional singer. A good quality singing voice, combined with a prayerful approach to the psalmody, will lift the people in prayer much better than a perfect singing voice that appears more as performance than prayer. Cantors need to hone those skills that make for greater knowledge of music in general and to familiarize themselves with the musical settings which generally differ from the hymns and songs to which we are more accustomed. Cantors sing the antiphon in such a way that every member of the assembly feels welcome to join when it is introduced and repeated. This means inviting people to sing the refrain at the appropriate time. A raised hand and eye contact express this invitation well. Those gathered are not an audience, but the assembly of God's people who respond to God's word.

The cantor's second important task is to know the psalmody, especially that used in morning and evening prayer. This is important for all who exercise leadership in liturgical prayer and for all who gather to share in this action of worship. In the section on the psalmody, we discussed some of its different approaches, such as praise, thanksgiving, intercession, penitence and conversion. At times two or more of these approaches to prayer are found in the same psalm. While the musical setting may not vary, awareness of such a change enables both cantor and assembly to enter into the prayer more fully.

The Minister of the Word (Reader)

Because one scripture reading is part of the celebration, there is a role for the minister of the word. Whenever the word of God is proclaimed in the liturgical assembly, we acknowledge that our God is speaking to us. This is true of both the celebration of eucharist and all liturgical prayer. Following the third psalm or the canticle, the reader comes forward to proclaim the chosen text. This pericope (a term used in biblical studies for a passage of scripture consisting of a few verses that normally has a central theme or message) is taken from either the Jewish or Christian scriptures (Old or New Testament), but it is not a gospel text. The gospels proclaimed in morning and evening prayer are the canticles of Zechariah and Mary, respectively.

The reader does not normally process in with the Lectionary as in a celebration of the word or mass, although some outlines for this prayer indicate that the Lectionary is carried in a procession. The Canadian ritual book, *Sunday Celebration of the Word and Hours*, makes this procession an important part of the gathering rites in a community that cannot celebrate the eucharist on Sunday; therefore it is not the norm. In such cases, there is an extended liturgy of the word as part of the prayer; a homily is also given. In general, however, morning and evening prayer emphasize praise, thanksgiving and intercession; thus I recommend that there be no procession with the Lectionary.

Still, the quality of the proclamation is very important. All members of the assembly need to not only hear the message clearly, but acknowledge it as proclamation, as God's living word speaking to us in the depths of our beings. Therefore, there is nothing casual about the role of the reader here or at any liturgical celebration.

The Thurifer

This ministry is one of silent leadership. It requires graceful movement and the ability to move through the assembly without drawing attention to oneself to allow those present to encounter with the holy through the fragrance of burning incense. The thurifer leads the procession in evening prayer, carrying either the traditional thurible or a bowl with lighted charcoal. Incense is placed on the coals during the singing of the evening psalm and the thurifer incenses both people and objects as the gospel canticle is sung. You'll find more details on this in the section on evening prayer, pages 34-35.

In Summary

1. Gathering to praise our God and intercede for the church and world is an essential part of the Christian vocation. To allow this gathering to take place with reverence and care, a variety of ministries are required.

2. Though requiring a variety of gifts and skills, these different liturgical roles are important as they serve the assembly.

Discussion Questions

1. Does your community have a process for discerning different ministries, liturgical and otherwise? What are the essential qualities of every minister in public prayer?

2. Two requirements of all liturgical ministers are an attitude of loving service for the community and an openness to new ways of performing ministry. How are you able to assure this in your community? What skills are needed in the formation process?

CHAPTER 5

Symbols and Rituals for Morning and Evening Prayer

Morning Prayer

The community gathers in the morning for prayer to praise God for a new day. It is a time to acknowledge the beauty of creation and gift of life we have through Christ, the risen Lord. Perhaps the most powerful symbol of morning prayer is the gift of light from the sun. The second one is the assembly itself, gathered to give praise. Therefore, morning prayer does not normally use candles or other symbolic objects. Some exceptions may be the paschal candle during the Easter season and an incense bowl on a special feast. These would have a greater impact in communities where morning prayer takes place on a regular basis.

This prayer needs no formal procession. The presider, assistant and cantor go to their seats a few minutes before the prayer begins. When all have gathered, the ministers stand (on cue from the presider) and the assembly does the same. The opening greeting is just that, the symbolic first words of the day that offer praise: "Lord, open our lips ... and we shall proclaim your praise." All present make a sign of the cross on their lips at the opening words.

A morning hymn such as "O God of Light" (*CBW III*, 13C) follows. This musical setting, which dates back to the seventeenth century, is always a good choice. *CBW III* offers many good alternatives; nineteen are listed in the index. Some are well known, while others may appear quite different at first. It is always good to begin with the familiar, but don't stay there. Rich lyrics and music contain a treasure that God's people should have the opportunity to use in prayer.

The traditional morning psalm is Psalm 63, sometimes entitled, "Your Love is Finer Than Life." *CBW III* offers four settings for this psalm; the first is 13D in the morning prayer format; others are found at numbers 656-658. Some translations of this psalm refer very specifically to the morning, while others, for instance, that of the *NRSV*, translate that verse differently. This prayer calls on God, acknowledging that God's love is better than life itself. We pray this cry for deliverance from our enemies with the assurance that God, who has been there in the past, will continue to be our help.

Evening Prayer

The symbols and rituals of evening prayer help the community come together for worship and recognize more clearly their vocation to offer praise to God and intercede for the world.

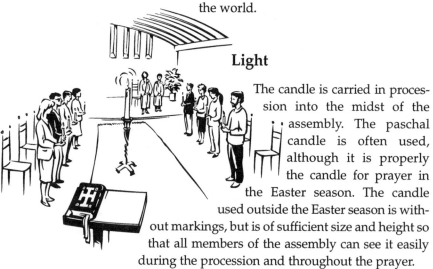

Light

The candle is carried in procession into the midst of the assembly. The paschal candle is often used, although it is properly the candle for prayer in the Easter season. The candle used outside the Easter season is without markings, but is of sufficient size and height so that all members of the assembly can see it easily during the procession and throughout the prayer.

There are some practical matters to care for here. Be sure that the stand is a good height so that the assistant can easily place the candle in it with relative ease. The best setup is to have the candle already fitted into a sleeve that slides snugly into the base. When such movements happen gracefully and without a struggle, everyone is more at ease and can enter more readily into the prayer.

For the service of light, give all participants tapers as they enter. Then, after the candle has been put in place, they can receive the light, which is spread throughout the assembly and kept burning at least during the evening thanksgiving and hymn.

Incense

Incense is used as a sign of our prayer rising to God. Its roots are in the temple worship where an incense sacrifice was offered. During the incense psalm (Psalm 141), the assistant or presider places some incense on the coals; its smoke rises before us. During the gospel canticle, the assembly, candle and possibly the Lectionary are incensed indicating our respect for these liturgical symbols and for one another.

The use of incense is becoming problematic in evening prayer as well as in other liturgical celebrations. There are attempts to find non-allergenic types of incense, among other solutions to this problem, but to date few are satisfactory. Does the use of incense and chemically treated charcoal for easy lighting have a greater priority than keeping some members away from community prayer? Do we let go of a traditional symbol because our modern world has not been able to keep the earth and atmosphere in a healthy state? I have no definitive answer to this problem, but I do believe that we must keep the well-being of the members of the community as the higher priority. In the remainder of this book, the use of incense will be addressed as a regular part of the prayer; liturgical preparation teams will need to make their own choices regarding this particular issue.

Symbols and Gestures
for Both Morning and Evening Prayer

Lectionary

Because this is not a liturgy of the word, it does not give the same emphasis to the Lectionary as does eucharist or a celebration of the word.

The choice of reading depends on the situation. For Sunday evenings, one possibility is the second reading of the mass, which, in Ordinary Time, may not be directly related to the first reading and gospel. Therefore the community has another opportunity to hear this reading; a short homily would bring its message into the life of the assembly. The first reading from weekday Lectionary and the readings from *The Prayer of the Church* or *Christian Prayer* (Catholic Book Publishing Company, New York, 1976) are good sources that keep us in touch with the seasons and feasts. Gospel readings are normally not used at evening or morning prayer since the two canticles, of Zechariah (Luke 1:68-79) and of Mary (Luke 1:46-55), provide the gospel readings announced, not in the traditional manner, but as a sung proclamation of the whole assembly.

Vesture

The standard vesture for all liturgical ministers is the alb, symbol of the new life given in baptism. When presider, assistant, cantor and thurifer are robed in similarly-styled albs, they represent the whole baptised community called to praise and intercession. For larger groups in the parish church or other chapel, the alb is especially appropriate. The only addition to this is the stole worn by an ordained presider. There is no need for crosses, capes or other inventions. Simplicity and grace make the alb an effective symbol for the whole assembly.

Procession

The prayer begins with thurifer, candle bearer, cantor, [lector] and presider coming into the assembly in semi-darkness. All turn toward the light and respond to the opening proclamation. At this time, the light is passed through the assembly so all can light their tapers. The cantor or assistant now proclaims the thanksgiving for light (for example, *CBW III*, 14E). This is followed immediately by the evening hymn (*CBW III*, 14G or another chosen for the season or feast).

Standing

All stand from the beginning until the end of the hymn. As the presider sits, the assembly does likewise and extinguishes its candles. The lights are turned on.

When the presider stands to lead the people in a kind of collect prayer after each of the psalms, the whole assembly does the same. The assembly remains standing during the canticle of praise which follows immediately after the prayer of the second psalm.

Following a period of silence after the reading (and homily), on cue from the presider, the assembly stands for the gospel canticle and remains in that posture for the duration of the prayer.

Sitting

The members of the assembly are seated following the hymn for the psalmody, the reading and the homily. The posture of sitting during the psalmody has a slightly different meaning than during the reading and homily. It is a prayerful moment guided by the cantor in a spirit of openness to the way the Lord speaks to us through the words of the psalm.

Bowing

The assembly may bow if it is standing when the doxology "Glory to the Father and to the Son and to the Holy Spirit" is sung. It appears a little awkward to bow when seated, though some groups do so gracefully. When the thurifer incenses the assembly, members bow as the smoke of the incense is directed towards them. This bow is a gesture of acceptance of being a member of God's holy people gathered in prayer.

Sign of peace

Evening prayer usually ends with an exchange of the sign of peace, expressed according to local custom. There is usually no formal ending after the sign of peace. The ministers mingle with the assembly and, after an appropriate time, all disperse.

A Lenten Option

The Cross

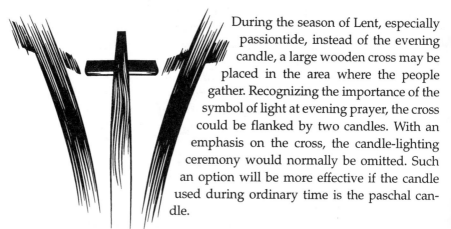

During the season of Lent, especially passiontide, instead of the evening candle, a large wooden cross may be placed in the area where the people gather. Recognizing the importance of the symbol of light at evening prayer, the cross could be flanked by two candles. With an emphasis on the cross, the candle-lighting ceremony would normally be omitted. Such an option will be more effective if the candle used during ordinary time is the paschal candle.

Evening Prayer in the Order of Christian Funerals

The *Order of Christian Funerals* is the book containing the different liturgical rites for funerals in Canada. Of the eleven vigil services for adults, nine of them are celebrations of the word. The two evening prayer options allow a different style of prayer at the funeral home or parish church.

These are probably the less frequently used options for the service at the funeral home or at the parish church. They deserve more attention, especially in a vigil for someone who has been involved in the faith community. Because there is a participant's book, it is possible to use the format with little need to make additions. This prayer is also a good option if prayers are celebrated on two different evenings. As in every liturgical celebration, evening prayer at the funeral vigil requires well-prepared ministers who can adapt to the circumstances of the funeral home. This includes the ministry of consolation for the family members and friends who are grieving. Good ritual prayer in all parts of the funeral liturgy allows those who grieve to have something to lean on and carry them when other words may fail. As well, music and song are especially important for all involved. Do not hesitate to use this prayer for the funeral vigil.

In Summary

1. The pastoral office requires a number of symbols and gestures in order to express fully the nature of the prayer. The symbols of alb, light and incense and the gestures of procession, standing, sitting, bowing, signing oneself, and sharing the kiss of peace take the prayer beyond words to a ritual action incorporating the different senses.

2. Different liturgical seasons (i.e. Lent and Easter), and special celebrations (funeral vigils) may require adaptations not only of the hymn, psalms and intercessions, but also in the use of gestures and symbols such as candle and cross.

Discussion Questions

1. Two tendencies in liturgy are minimalism and triumphalism (over-acting). Discuss ways to avoid these in your use of the gestures and symbols that you read about in this chapter.

2. The use of vesture such as albs requires practice in movement and gesture. Are the leaders of prayer comfortable wearing albs? Discuss the need for practice with this and other aspects of the prayer.

3. Is incense used regularly in the liturgy in your community? Does its use prohibit some people from taking part in the public prayer of the church? How do we continue to be a welcoming community while using these treasured symbols? Are there other options?

Celebrating as God's People

Different names are given to this morning and evening prayer: lauds and vespers, the cathedral or pastoral office, morning praise and evening thanksgiving. One that I find appealing is the pastoral office, for it is prayer that is especially suited to the parish community as a regular form of liturgical prayer.

But titles or names are not really important. The task we are given as liturgical leaders is to bring this prayer into the regular practice of the life of the church. This requires good planning, positive promotion and joyful celebration in our parishes and every other place where we have the opportunity to gather for prayer. It means that we need to be able to adapt to different circumstances and be willing to call forth those people with the skills and gifts required to make this prayer a reality throughout the church.

Ultimately, this prayer needs faith as its solid basis: faith in God's presence in our lives and world, a faith based on hope and lived in love. Our willingness to gather our people to pray in this way is a tangible sign of our love for them. When we have made steps in this direction, I am certain that we will celebrate better who we are as God's people, immersed into the death and resurrection of Jesus Christ. The morning and evening pastoral office, like all prayer, will naturally lead us to the fuller celebration of our faith at the banquet of the eucharist.

Morning Prayer Planning Sheet

Date: _____ Day: _____

Feast or Season: _____

Ministers

Presider: _____

Cantor: _____

Lector: _____

Assistant: _____

Alb (or other Vesture)
Yes:_____ No: _____

Format

Morning hymn: _____

First psalm [psalm 63]: _____

Prayer by presider: _____

Second psalm: _____

Prayer by presider: _____

Canticle of praise:_____

Word of God: _____

Gospel canticle [Benedictus]: _____

Intercessions:
prepared: _____ spontaneous: _____
sung: _____ spoken: _____

Response to the intercessions: _____

Our Father:
sung: _____ spoken: _____

Closing prayer by presider: _____

Blessing:_____

Sign of Peace: _____

Evening Prayer Planning Sheet

Date: _____ Day: _____

Feast or Season:_____

Ministers

Presider: _____

Cantor: _____

Lector:_____

Thurifer: _____

Assistant [Candle bearer]: _____

Vesture (Alb or other)
Yes _____ No_____

Format

Procession with candle: _____

Proclamation of light [opening greeting]: _____

Evening thanksgiving:_____

Evening hymn: _____

First psalm [incense psalm or other]: _____

Prayer by presider: _____

Second psalm: _____

Prayer by presider: _____

Canticle of praise:_____

Word of God:_____

Gospel canticle [Magnificat]: _____

Intercessions
Prepared _____ Spontaneous _____
Sung _____ Spoken_____

Response to the Intercessions: _____

Our Father [sung or spoken]:_____

Closing prayer by presider: _____

Blessing: _____

Sign of Peace: _____

PRAISE IS YOURS, O GOD, FOREVER

Te Deum laudamus

1.Praise is yours, O God, for - ev - er; yours all hom - age,
2.Glo - ry- crown'd a - pos - tles praise you, white- robed mar - tyrs
3.You, O Christ, en - throned tri - um- phant, God the Fa - ther's
4.Come, Lord Je - sus, save your peo - ple, bless the flock you

Lord, a - lone. Earth it - self, e - ter - nal Fa - ther
shout your name. Pro - phet voic - es give you hon - our,
on - ly Son, scorn - ing not our hum - an na - ture,
call your own. Day by day we sound your prai - ses,

bows in awe be - fore your throne. An - gel pow - ers
earth - ly church joins loud ac - claim. Praise is yours, al -
death de - feat - ed, vic - t'ry won. By your blood you
ev - er - more your name make known. Keep us al - ways

sound your glo - ry: Ho - ly, Ho - ly God of hosts!
migh - ty Fa - ther, with the Son, and Spi- rit One,
brought re- demp - tion: Grant us glo - ry with your saints.
in your mer - cy: Lord, in you our hope is sure.

Ho - ly, Ho - ly God of hosts!
with the Son, and Spi - rit one.
Grant us glo - ry with your saints.
Lord, in you our hope is sure.

Music: John Hughes 1873-1932, CWM RHONDDA 87878 and repeat
Words: © 1996, Raymond J. Lahey.

GLOSSARY

Alb: simple white robe that covers the person from shoulder to ankle as well as the arms: a baptismal robe symbolizing new life and purity.

Antiphonal: refers to a style of music that features a verse or refrain which is alternated between two groups of singers.

Assembly: the Latin word *ecclesia* may be translated as "assembly" or "church." Denotes an officially-convoked gathering; generally preferred to "congregation." The Christian assembly is convoked by the risen and glorious Lord.

Benedictus: Zechariah's song from Luke 1:68-79; the traditional canticle for Morning Prayer.

Canticle: a non-metrical song, usually from scripture, that is to be sung, e.g. Magnificat, Gloria, Benedictus, Te Deum.

Lauds: traditional name for morning prayer composed of a hymn, psalms, canticles and intercessions with a focus on praise of God and resurrection.

Magnificat: Mary's song from Luke 1:46-55; the traditional canticle for evening prayer.

Paschal (Easter) candle: large decorated candle first lit at the Easter Vigil, and used throughout the season, as well as at baptisms and funerals.

Psalmody: book of the Jewish scriptures containing 150 psalms with themes of praise, lament and thanksgiving. They are central to the liturgy of the hours.

Responsorial: a method of singing, especially of the psalms, in which the verses are sung by a solo voice (cantor), and the choir and congregation sing the refrain after each verse.

Ritual: actions and words of a community at prayer that, through repetition and a predictable pattern, permit the community to encounter God and experience salvation.

Te Deum: hymn of praise that begins *Te Deum laudamus*, "We praise you, O God"; used during the liturgy of the hours, especially on Sundays and Feast Days when the "Glory to God" is used at eucharist.

Thurible: a container, usually metal or pottery, in which burning charcoal and incense are placed, causing smoke to rise as a symbol of prayer.

Vespers: a term for the evening prayer of the church, composed of a hymn, psalms, canticles and intercessions. It focuses on thanksgiving and a plea for forgiveness.

BIBLIOGRAPHY

Recommended Reading

Bradshaw, Paul F. *Daily Prayer in the Early Church.* New York: Oxford University Press, 1982. This is a good book for those who wish to study the history of liturgical prayer from its roots in Judaism and the different Christian expressions in the first centuries.

Bradshaw, Paul F. *Two Ways of Praying.* Nashville: Abingdon Press, 1995. In his second book, Bradshaw discusses the differences between monastic and cathedral offices. He includes some very helpful reading on christology, psalmody and other scripture readings. The book also offers an outline for prayer.

Gallen, John S.J., editor. *Christians at Prayer.* Notre Dame, IN: University of Notre Dame Press, 1977. Besides Gallen's introduction, there are eight articles by liturgists and other theologians from a variety of Christian traditions. A good review of different aspects of liturgical prayer.

Guiver, George. *Company of Voices, Daily Prayer and the People of God.* New York: Pueblo Publishing Company, 1988. Guiver describes his book as a historical overview of the practice of prayer in the Christian church. It is a good source of information spanning the centuries. It is contemporary and worth reading for those who wish to know more about the background of modern liturgical prayer.

Jungman, Joseph A. *Christian Prayer Through the Centuries.* New York: Paulist Press, 1978. Although this book is a little dated, it is always worthwhile to read a work by Joseph Jungman. This historical overview will help you understand our roots in Christian prayer.

Roguet, A.-M., O.P. *The Liturgy of the Hours, The General Instruction and Commentary.* Collegeville: The Liturgical Press, 1971. This book contains both the liturgical document and reflections by the author. Good background information.

Shepherd, Massey H., Jr. *The Psalms in Christian Worship, A Practical Guide*. Minneapolis: Augsburg, 1976. To gain a deeper insight into the different types of psalmody as well as their use in Christian prayer, this book is quite helpful.

Taft, Robert, S.J. *The Liturgy of the Hours in East and West*. Collegeville: The Liturgical Press, 1986. This scholarly book is rich in the history of liturgical prayer and covers in detail how it developed in different geographical areas. For those who wish to do a more thorough study of the church's prayer, this book will be most helpful.

Catholic Book of Worship III. Ottawa: Publications Service, Canadian Conference of Catholic Bishops, 1994. This liturgical book is the standard for the Canadian Church and hopefully will be one of the principal vehicles for our recovering the beauty of morning and evening prayer.

Order of Christian Funerals. Ottawa: Publications Service, Canadian Conference of Catholic Bishops, 1990. The two formats for evening prayer and vigil services are especially our concern here. There is also a model for morning and evening prayer based on the breviary format titled "Office for the Dead," pages 347 to 377 (Part IV).

Praise God in Song, Ecumenical Daily Prayer. Chicago: G.I.A. Publications, 1979. This book was designed for a broad Christian usage. The formats and psalm translations are a little dated but it continues to be a good resource for both the principles and formats of daily prayer.

Pray without Ceasing: Prayer for Morning and Evening. Collegeville, MN: The Liturgical Press, 1993. With a simpler structure than the official Roman rite for the liturgy of the hours, this prayer is accessible for all who pray the hours. *Pray without Ceasing* renews the intent of morning and evening prayer as the prayer of the whole church.

Psalms for the Liturgical Year: Music for the NRSV Psalter. Musical settings by Gordon Johnston. Ottawa: Novalis, 1997. Above-average music for the average congregation. The first-ever musical settings of the psalms of the Lectionary published by the Canadian Conference of Catholic Bishops. Four volumes, Years A, B, C and Feasts, Seasons and Common Psalms.

Psalms for Morning and Evening Prayer. Chicago: Liturgical Training Publications, 1995. This is a prayer book that will be of great use in either personal or communal prayer. The ICEL committee has made great strides in the poetic expression of the psalms and offers a well-planned book for their use in daily prayer.

Sunday Celebration of the Word and Hours. Ottawa: Publications Service, Canadian Conference of Catholic Bishops, 1995. This ritual book is designed for celebrations on Sunday when the eucharist cannot be celebrated. On pages 242 and following are formats for morning and evening prayer designed for use specifically on Sunday. The formats, however, can be adapted for use at other times. The psalm prayers within the rites and on pages 331-335 and other presidential prayers in the book are a helpful resource for liturgical planning committees.

Work of God: Benedictine Prayer. Collegeville, MN: The Liturgical Press, 1997. While published primarily for Benedictine Oblates, this prayerbook gives the user a starting place in praying the Liturgy of the Hours. Largely a two-week arrangement of morning and evening prayer, it also provides an introduction to monastic spirituality and its relevance for non-monastics.